Can You See Sasha?

by Katie Dale
illustrated by Ian Smith

OXFORD
UNIVERSITY PRESS

Seth can not see Sasha the cat.

That is not Sasha.
It is a quick chick!

Seth dashes to the bank.
He sees a big toad.

I think Sasha is
in the rushes!

It is not Sasha.
It is a duck!

A robin sings high in the oak.

Then Seth sees a tail.

It is not Sasha.
It is Buzz the dog!

Seth checks the sink and bath.

Then he checks his bed.

“I can not see my cat,” sighs Seth.

I can see
a cat!

Seth peeps at the cat.

No, it is a kitten!

Can you see Sasha?
Yes, I can!

toad

duck

chick

robin

Encourage students to read the animal names and match them to the pictures.